Simple *but* Sarcastic
Gratitude
JOURNAL

Created by
Bee Byrd

This Journal Belongs To:

_____

Everyone else keep your grubby hands off.

About this *journal*...

Sometimes life sucks. It's really hard to come up with flowery positive words when life is kicking you in the gut. Depending on your path in life, you might want to punch a wall or you might just naturally leak sarcasm. No matter where you are in life, this journal is here to help.

Gratitude is important. It's the thing that helps us keep hope in humanity when humans are being stupid - *and sometimes they are really stupid.* A huge gift of gratitude is the fact that it shows us that we are enough. You might be thankful for the way your hair sticks up on end or the way that you overcame a huge obstacle. No matter what, you're amazing and you're enough. List it out and be proud.

Gratitude also helps us be thankful for the life that is lived around us, even the tiny things we take for granted. Naming what we are thankful in our lives is a powerful tool. Little by little, you might find yourself wanting less and cherishing what you already hold.

This journal was created to acknowledge gratitude every day while also providing a place to briefly vent about what really sucked. It's a brilliant give and take approach (*If we say so ourselves*). Week-by-week you can write down things you're thankful for but also pause to pat yourself on the back for not letting the air out of someone's tires (*well done you!*).

By the end of this journal, what are you hoping to achieve? ⬎

How to use this *journal*...

Using this journal is simple.

- There's 6 months worth of weekly pages to fill out. Every day fill in the appropriate day and then at the end of the week, fill in the emoticons at the top right corner to represent your overall week. Hopefully over time, as you're listing out what you're thankful for, you'll see your moods start to trend upward.

- You're the expert for your life. That's why you get to choose how to use the weekly pages of this journal. Every day there's a small space to fill out what you're thankful for on that day. You can list one thing on each of the 4 lines or you can just use the space to freely write. It's up to you.

- After you fill in what you're thankful for each day, don't forget to express what really sucked. Hopefully you can leave the crappy parts on the page and move forward feeling a little bit freer.

- Behind the weekly journal pages are several free writing journal pages with gratitude prompts. Use this section wisely, *or don't...* it's up to you. Free writing is a great exercise for times when maybe you're not feeling overcome with gratitude (such as when hopeful politicians start knocking on your door).

- Toward the very end of this journal there are several free writing pages without journal prompts. (*No, we didn't just get lazy.*) This section is for you to fill in your own prompts. Maybe you want to focus on diving deeper on your gratitude journey or maybe your bossy therapist asked you to write about why you're thankful for not throat punching someone. You're free to fill in your own prompts and then get to work expressing your gratefulness.

Now get to work! And be thankful!

Simple things to be *thankful* for...

- green grass
- you favorite song
- soft sheets
- best friends
- soothing candles
- sunsets
- steady jobs
- learning new skills
- falling leaves
- meaningful gifts
- family
- dancing together
- your favorite pen
- a delicious meal
- supportive people
- cool breezes
- being warm
- clean towels
- grocery stores
- lazy saturdays
- loveable pets
- caring texts
- small victories

- modern medicine
- apple pie
- snowball fights
- crazy cousins
- reaching goals
- refreshing rain
- fresh food
- messy art supplie
- clean water
- christmas gifts
- strong leadership
- loveable pets
- funny jokes
- caring texts
- hiking or yoga
- lights that work
- colorful flowers
- technology
- hiking or yoga
- lights that work
- colorful flowers
- technology
- genuine smiles

Simple things to be *despised*...

- politician's hairstyles
- colonoscopies
- an empty cookie box
- broken toilets
- cliffhangers
- group texts
- price of mattresses
- annoying mosquitos
- going to the bathroom without a phone
- dog farts
- remembering passwords
- when the garbage bag tears
- paper straws
- WiFi passwords with 94 characters
- food poisoning
- algebra
- Cowboy fans
- slimey sponges
- flying cockroaches
- wet toilet seats
- slow internet connections
- Monday mornings
- stepping in cat puke

Week of: _____ How was this week? 😨 😕 😐 🙂 😎

Today I am grateful for ↴   Today's Date:

| |
| |
| |
| |

But this totally sucks:

Today I am grateful for ↴   Today's Date:

| |
| |
| |
| |

But this totally sucks:

Today I am grateful for ↴   Today's Date:

| |
| |
| |
| |

But this totally sucks:

"It's not happiness that brings us gratitude. It's gratitude that brings us happiness." — Anonymous

Great. But can it bring coffee?

Today I am grateful for ↴   Today's Date:

But this totally sucks:

Today I am grateful for ↴   Today's Date:

But this totally sucks:

Today I am grateful for ↴   Today's Date:

But this totally sucks:

Today I am grateful for ↴   Today's Date:

But this totally sucks:

Week of: _____ How was this week? 😟 😕 😐 🙂 😎

Today I am grateful for ↴   Today's Date:

But this totally sucks:

Today I am grateful for ↴   Today's Date:

But this totally sucks:

Today I am grateful for ↴   Today's Date:

But this totally sucks:

Staying Positive.

That it will all go horribly wrong.

Today I am grateful for ⬎   Today's Date:

| |
| |
| |
| |

But this totally sucks:

Today I am grateful for ⬎   Today's Date:

| |
| |
| |
| |

But this totally sucks:

Today I am grateful for ⬎   Today's Date:

| |
| |
| |
| |

But this totally sucks:

Today I am grateful for ⬎   Today's Date:

| |
| |
| |
| |

But this totally sucks:

Week of: _____   How was this week? 😨 🙁 😳 🙂 😎

Today I am grateful for ↴   Today's Date:

| |
| |
| |
| |

But this totally sucks:

Today I am grateful for ↴   Today's Date:

| |
| |
| |
| |

But this totally sucks:

Today I am grateful for ↴   Today's Date:

| |
| |
| |
| |

But this totally sucks:

When life gives you lemons,

throw them at someone.

Today I am grateful for ↴   Today's Date:

But this totally sucks:

Today I am grateful for ↴   Today's Date:

But this totally sucks:

Today I am grateful for ↴   Today's Date:

But this totally sucks:

Today I am grateful for ↴   Today's Date:

But this totally sucks:

Week of: _____   How was this week? 😫 🙁 😐 🙂 😄

Today I am grateful for ↴   Today's Date:

But this totally sucks:

Today I am grateful for ↴   Today's Date:

But this totally sucks:

Today I am grateful for ↴   Today's Date:

But this totally sucks:

"Due to recent cut backs, the light at the
end of the tunnel has been
turned off."

Today I am grateful for ⮧   Today's Date:

But this totally sucks:

Today I am grateful for ⮧   Today's Date:

But this totally sucks:

Today I am grateful for ⮧   Today's Date:

But this totally sucks:

Today I am grateful for ⮧   Today's Date:

But this totally sucks:

Week of: _____ How was this week? 😲 😕 😬 🙂 😎

Today I am grateful for ⤵   Today's Date:

| |
| |
| |
| |

But this totally sucks:

Today I am grateful for ⤵   Today's Date:

| |
| |
| |
| |

But this totally sucks:

Today I am grateful for ⤵   Today's Date:

| |
| |
| |
| |

But this totally sucks:

> "There is always, always, always something to be grateful for,"
>
> *said the person who was not hugging a toilet at 3am.*

Today I am grateful for ↴   Today's Date:

But this totally sucks:

Today I am grateful for ↴   Today's Date:

But this totally sucks:

Today I am grateful for ↴   Today's Date:

But this totally sucks:

Today I am grateful for ↴   Today's Date:

But this totally sucks:

Week of: _____   How was this week? 😵 😕 😌 ☺ 😎

Today I am grateful for ↴   Today's Date:

| |
| |
| |
| |

But this totally sucks:

Today I am grateful for ↴   Today's Date:

| |
| |
| |
| |

But this totally sucks:

Today I am grateful for ↴   Today's Date:

| |
| |
| |
| |

But this totally sucks:

I am a person who wants to do a lot of things,

trapped in the body of someone who wants to sleep a lot.

Today I am grateful for ⬎   Today's Date:

But this totally sucks:

Today I am grateful for ⬎   Today's Date:

But this totally sucks:

Today I am grateful for ⬎   Today's Date:

But this totally sucks:

Today I am grateful for ⬎   Today's Date:

But this totally sucks:

Week of: _____ How was this week? 😟 😕 😌 🙂 😎

Today I am grateful for ↴   Today's Date:

| |
| |
| |
| |

But this totally sucks:

Today I am grateful for ↴   Today's Date:

| |
| |
| |
| |

But this totally sucks:

Today I am grateful for ↴   Today's Date:

| |
| |
| |
| |

But this totally sucks:

Gratitude turns what we have into enough.

Can someone please tell this to my bank account?

Today I am grateful for ↴   Today's Date:

But this totally sucks:

Today I am grateful for ↴   Today's Date:

But this totally sucks:

Today I am grateful for ↴   Today's Date:

But this totally sucks:

Today I am grateful for ↴   Today's Date:

But this totally sucks:

Week of: _____ How was this week? 😟 🙁 😐 🙂 😎

Today I am grateful for ⮧   Today's Date:

| |
| |
| |
| |

But this totally sucks:

Today I am grateful for ⮧   Today's Date:

| |
| |
| |
| |

But this totally sucks:

Today I am grateful for ⮧   Today's Date:

| |
| |
| |
| |

But this totally sucks:

You deserve a medal for making it through this week without stabbing somebody with a fork.

Be thankful for that.

Today I am grateful for ⤵   Today's Date:

But this totally sucks:

Today I am grateful for ⤵   Today's Date:

But this totally sucks:

Today I am grateful for ⤵   Today's Date:

But this totally sucks:

Today I am grateful for ⤵   Today's Date:

But this totally sucks:

Week of: _____ How was this week? 😣 😕 😌 🙂 😎

Today I am grateful for ⤵   Today's Date:

| |
| |
| |
| |

But this totally sucks:

Today I am grateful for ⤵   Today's Date:

| |
| |
| |
| |

But this totally sucks:

Today I am grateful for ⤵   Today's Date:

| |
| |
| |
| |

But this totally sucks:

"A moment of gratitude makes a difference in your attitude."

I'm just looking for something to keep me out of jail.

Today I am grateful for ↴   Today's Date:

But this totally sucks:

Today I am grateful for ↴   Today's Date:

But this totally sucks:

Today I am grateful for ↴   Today's Date:

But this totally sucks:

Today I am grateful for ↴   Today's Date:

But this totally sucks:

Week of: _____   How was this week? ☹ 😕 😐 🙂 😎

Today I am grateful for ↴   Today's Date:

| |
| |
| |
| |

But this totally sucks:

Today I am grateful for ↴   Today's Date:

| |
| |
| |
| |

But this totally sucks:

Today I am grateful for ↴   Today's Date:

| |
| |
| |
| |

But this totally sucks:

"I feel a very unusual sensation - if it is not indigestion,
I think it must be gratitude."

Benjamin Disraeli

Today I am grateful for ⤵   Today's Date:

But this totally sucks:

Today I am grateful for ⤵   Today's Date:

But this totally sucks:

Today I am grateful for ⤵   Today's Date:

But this totally sucks:

Today I am grateful for ⤵   Today's Date:

But this totally sucks:

| Week of: _____ | How was this week? 😟 🙁 😌 ☺ 😎 |

Today I am grateful for ⬎   Today's Date:

But this totally sucks:

Today I am grateful for ⬎   Today's Date:

But this totally sucks:

Today I am grateful for ⬎   Today's Date:

But this totally sucks:

I want to say thank you to all the people who walked into my life
and made it outstanding,

and all the people who walked out of my life and
made it fantastic.

Today I am grateful for ↴   Today's Date:

But this totally sucks:

Today I am grateful for ↴   Today's Date:

But this totally sucks:

Today I am grateful for ↴   Today's Date:

But this totally sucks:

Today I am grateful for ↴   Today's Date:

But this totally sucks:

Week of: _____ How was this week? 😣 🙂 😌 ☺ 😎

Today I am grateful for ↴   Today's Date:

But this totally sucks:

Today I am grateful for ↴   Today's Date:

But this totally sucks:

Today I am grateful for ↴   Today's Date:

But this totally sucks:

Today I'm grateful.

Tomorrow? Now that might be a different story.

Today I am grateful for ↴   Today's Date:

But this totally sucks:

Today I am grateful for ↴   Today's Date:

But this totally sucks:

Today I am grateful for ↴   Today's Date:

But this totally sucks:

Today I am grateful for ↴   Today's Date:

But this totally sucks:

| Week of: _____ | How was this week? 😵 😕 😌 🙂 😎 |

Today I am grateful for ↴   Today's Date:

| |
| |
| |
| |

But this totally sucks:

Today I am grateful for ↴   Today's Date:

| |
| |
| |
| |

But this totally sucks:

Today I am grateful for ↴   Today's Date:

| |
| |
| |
| |

But this totally sucks:

They said not to give up on your dreams.

So I went back to sleep.

Today I am grateful for ↴   Today's Date:

But this totally sucks:

Today I am grateful for ↴   Today's Date:

But this totally sucks:

Today I am grateful for ↴   Today's Date:

But this totally sucks:

Today I am grateful for ↴   Today's Date:

But this totally sucks:

Week of: _____   How was this week? 😟 😕 😐 🙂 😎

Today I am grateful for ↴   Today's Date:

But this totally sucks:

Today I am grateful for ↴   Today's Date:

But this totally sucks:

Today I am grateful for ↴   Today's Date:

But this totally sucks:

"Life is a shipwreck but we must not forget to
sing in the lifeboats."

Voltaire

Today I am grateful for ↴   Today's Date:

But this totally sucks:

Today I am grateful for ↴   Today's Date:

But this totally sucks:

Today I am grateful for ↴   Today's Date:

But this totally sucks:

Today I am grateful for ↴   Today's Date:

But this totally sucks:

Week of: _____ How was this week? 😨 😕 😐 ☺ 😎

Today I am grateful for ↴   Today's Date:

| |
| |
| |
| |

But this totally sucks:

Today I am grateful for ↴   Today's Date:

| |
| |
| |
| |

But this totally sucks:

Today I am grateful for ↴   Today's Date:

| |
| |
| |
| |

But this totally sucks:

You never appreciate what you had until it's gone.

Toilet paper is a good example.

Today I am grateful for ↴   Today's Date:

But this totally sucks:

Today I am grateful for ↴   Today's Date:

But this totally sucks:

Today I am grateful for ↴   Today's Date:

But this totally sucks:

Today I am grateful for ↴   Today's Date:

But this totally sucks:

Week of: _____   How was this week? 😟 😕 😌 🙂 😎

Today I am grateful for ⤵   Today's Date:

| |
| |
| |
| |

But this totally sucks:

Today I am grateful for ⤵   Today's Date:

| |
| |
| |
| |

But this totally sucks:

Today I am grateful for ⤵   Today's Date:

| |
| |
| |
| |

But this totally sucks:

"God gave you a gift of 84,600 seconds today. Have you used one of them to say thank you?" – William Arthur Ward

I hope God didn't hear the other things I said today.

Today I am grateful for ⤵   Today's Date:

But this totally sucks:

Today I am grateful for ⤵   Today's Date:

But this totally sucks:

Today I am grateful for ⤵   Today's Date:

But this totally sucks:

Today I am grateful for ⤵   Today's Date:

But this totally sucks:

| Week of: _____ | How was this week? 😩 😕 😐 🙂 😎 |

Today I am grateful for ↴   Today's Date:

| |
| |
| |
| |

But this totally sucks:

Today I am grateful for ↴   Today's Date:

| |
| |
| |
| |

But this totally sucks:

Today I am grateful for ↴   Today's Date:

| |
| |
| |
| |

But this totally sucks:

I'm best served with coffee

and a side of sarcasm.

Today I am grateful for ↴   Today's Date:

But this totally sucks:

Today I am grateful for ↴   Today's Date:

But this totally sucks:

Today I am grateful for ↴   Today's Date:

But this totally sucks:

Today I am grateful for ↴   Today's Date:

But this totally sucks:

Week of: _____   How was this week? 😨 😕 😌 🙂 😎

Today I am grateful for ↴   Today's Date:

| |
| |
| |
| |

But this totally sucks:

Today I am grateful for ↴   Today's Date:

| |
| |
| |
| |

But this totally sucks:

Today I am grateful for ↴   Today's Date:

| |
| |
| |
| |

But this totally sucks:

The happiest people do not have the best of everything,

They make the best out of everything they have.

Today I am grateful for ⮑   Today's Date:

But this totally sucks:

Today I am grateful for ⮑   Today's Date:

But this totally sucks:

Today I am grateful for ⮑   Today's Date:

But this totally sucks:

Today I am grateful for ⮑   Today's Date:

But this totally sucks:

Week of: _____ How was this week? 😧 😕 😳 🙂 😎

Today I am grateful for ↴   Today's Date:

| |
| |
| |
| |

But this totally sucks:

Today I am grateful for ↴   Today's Date:

| |
| |
| |
| |

But this totally sucks:

Today I am grateful for ↴   Today's Date:

| |
| |
| |
| |

But this totally sucks:

When eating fruit, remember the one who planted the tree -
Vietnamese proverb

And don't forget all the crap that fertilized the tree.

Today I am grateful for ↴   Today's Date:

But this totally sucks:

Today I am grateful for ↴   Today's Date:

But this totally sucks:

Today I am grateful for ↴   Today's Date:

But this totally sucks:

Today I am grateful for ↴   Today's Date:

But this totally sucks:

Week of: _____ How was this week? 😧 😕 😌 ☺ 😎

Today I am grateful for ↴   Today's Date:

| |
| |
| |
| |

But this totally sucks:

Today I am grateful for ↴   Today's Date:

| |
| |
| |
| |

But this totally sucks:

Today I am grateful for ↴   Today's Date:

| |
| |
| |
| |

But this totally sucks:

An apple a day keeps anyone away.

If you throw it hard enough.

Today I am grateful for ↴   Today's Date:

But this totally sucks:

Today I am grateful for ↴   Today's Date:

But this totally sucks:

Today I am grateful for ↴   Today's Date:

But this totally sucks:

Today I am grateful for ↴   Today's Date:

But this totally sucks:

Week of: _____   How was this week? 😣 😕 😌 😊 😎

Today I am grateful for ↘   Today's Date:

But this totally sucks:

Today I am grateful for ↘   Today's Date:

But this totally sucks:

Today I am grateful for ↘   Today's Date:

But this totally sucks:

If each day is a gift,

I'd like to know where I can return Mondays.

Today I am grateful for ⌄   Today's Date:

But this totally sucks:

Today I am grateful for ⌄   Today's Date:

But this totally sucks:

Today I am grateful for ⌄   Today's Date:

But this totally sucks:

Today I am grateful for ⌄   Today's Date:

But this totally sucks:

Week of: _____ How was this week? 😒 🙁 😌 🙂 😎

Today I am grateful for ↴   Today's Date:

But this totally sucks:

Today I am grateful for ↴   Today's Date:

But this totally sucks:

Today I am grateful for ↴   Today's Date:

But this totally sucks:

I never make the same mistake twice.

I make it 5 or 6 times just to be sure.

Today I am grateful for ⤵   Today's Date:

But this totally sucks:

Today I am grateful for ⤵   Today's Date:

But this totally sucks:

Today I am grateful for ⤵   Today's Date:

But this totally sucks:

Today I am grateful for ⤵   Today's Date:

But this totally sucks:

| Week of: _____ | How was this week? 😣 🙁 😕 🙂 😎 |

Today I am grateful for ↴   Today's Date:

But this totally sucks:

Today I am grateful for ↴   Today's Date:

But this totally sucks:

Today I am grateful for ↴   Today's Date:

But this totally sucks:

"Understand your worth. Value your life. Appreciate your blessings."

"Know which friends will help you hide a body."

Today I am grateful for ⤵   Today's Date:

But this totally sucks:

Today I am grateful for ⤵   Today's Date:

But this totally sucks:

Today I am grateful for ⤵   Today's Date:

But this totally sucks:

Today I am grateful for ⤵   Today's Date:

But this totally sucks:

Week of: _____ How was this week? 😲 🙁 😌 🙂 😎

Today I am grateful for ↴   Today's Date:

But this totally sucks:

Today I am grateful for ↴   Today's Date:

But this totally sucks:

Today I am grateful for ↴   Today's Date:

But this totally sucks:

God gave us our relatives. Thank God we can choose our friends.

Ethel Watts Mumford

Today I am grateful for ↴   Today's Date:

But this totally sucks:

Today I am grateful for ↴   Today's Date:

But this totally sucks:

Today I am grateful for ↴   Today's Date:

But this totally sucks:

Today I am grateful for ↴   Today's Date:

But this totally sucks:

Week of: _____ How was this week? 😨 😕 😌 🙂 😎

Today I am grateful for ⬎   Today's Date:

| |
| |
| |
| |

But this totally sucks:

Today I am grateful for ⬎   Today's Date:

| |
| |
| |
| |

But this totally sucks:

Today I am grateful for ⬎   Today's Date:

| |
| |
| |
| |

But this totally sucks:

Two things I'm thankful for:

1. family and friends.
2. Caller ID to avoid family and friends.

Today I am grateful for ↴   Today's Date:

| |
| |
| |
| |
| But this totally sucks: |

Today I am grateful for ↴   Today's Date:

| |
| |
| |
| |
| But this totally sucks: |

Today I am grateful for ↴   Today's Date:

| |
| |
| |
| |
| But this totally sucks: |

Today I am grateful for ↴   Today's Date:

| |
| |
| |
| |
| But this totally sucks: |

Journal Prompt:

What is your secret gratitude? The one thing that you are most thankful for but no one else knows? Is it your favorite childhood cereal or how you love the smell of pencil erasers? Write it out. Your secret's safe here.

Date:

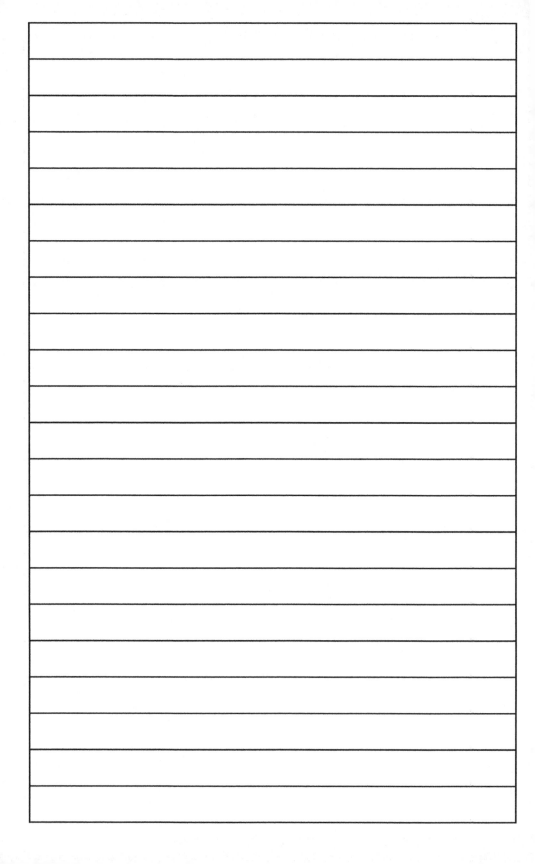

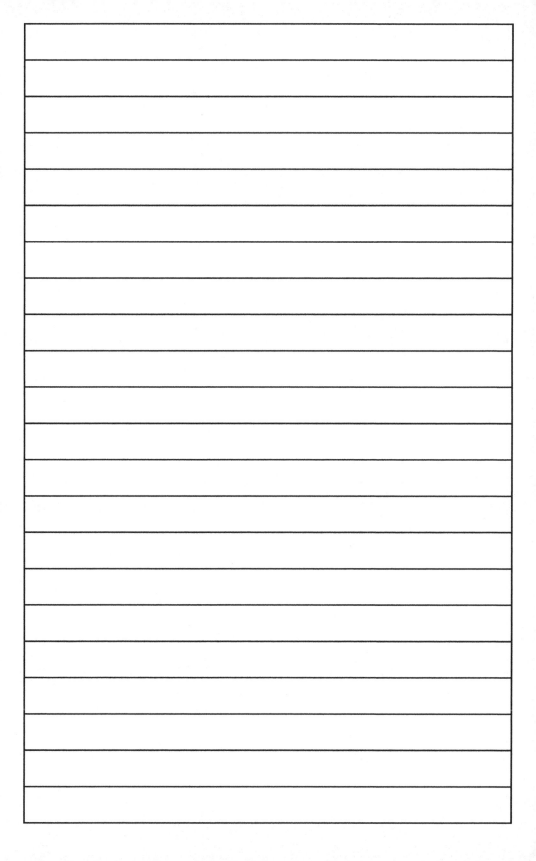

Journal Prompt:

Name 3 positive changes you've made in your life. But let's not stop there. Don't forget a quick sentence on why they sucked at the time but you're grateful for them now.

Date:

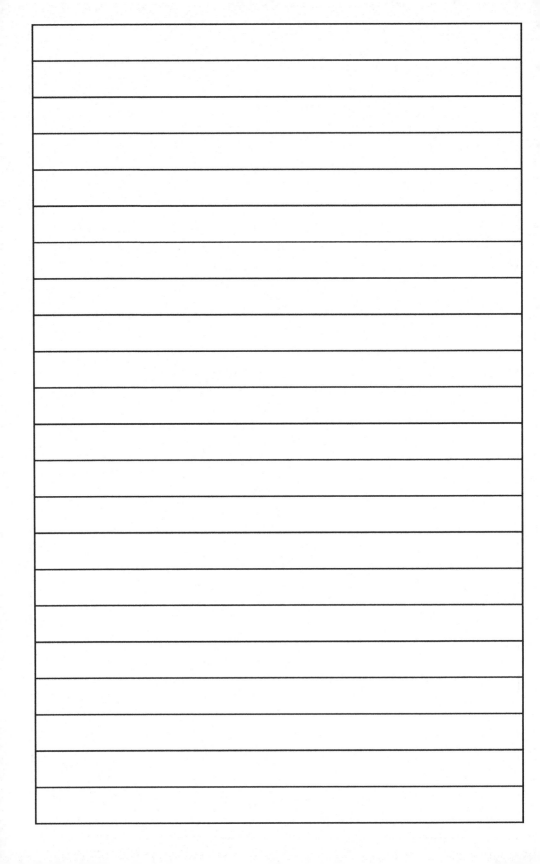

What is something you love about your family? Just a
reminder that the greatest family members are the ones
you don't want to throat punch and might not be blood
related. Sometimes friends equal true family.

Date:

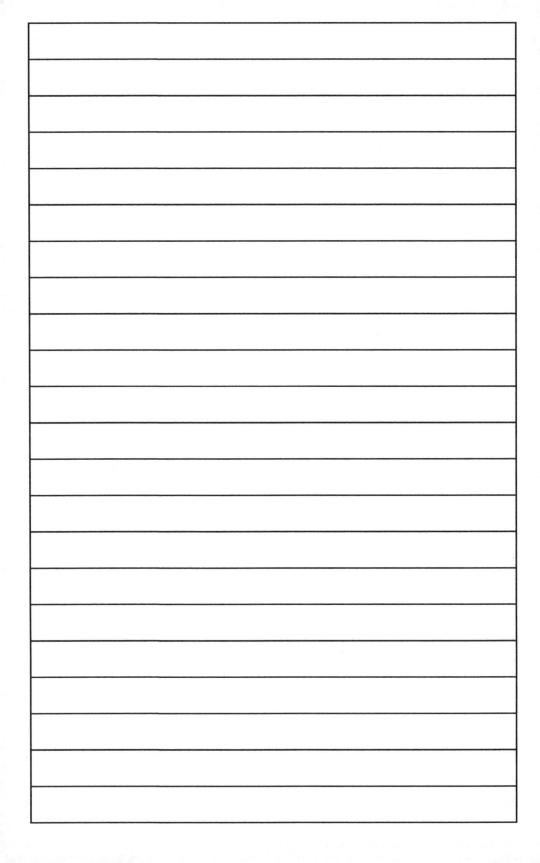

Journal Prompt:

If you could do the best day of your life over again,
what would it look like now? Would you line the road
with pink flamingos or salsa dance naked on the
beach?

Date:

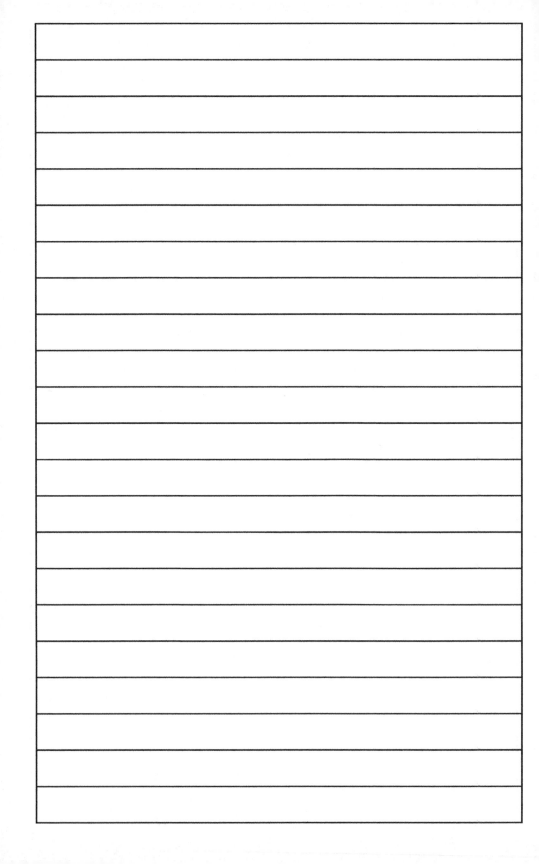

Journal Prompt:

What's the best thing that happened today? Maybe you overslept and then jumped into a pile of cat puke as you rushed to the shower...but it could have been worse, right? So what's the best thing that did happen and why?

Date:

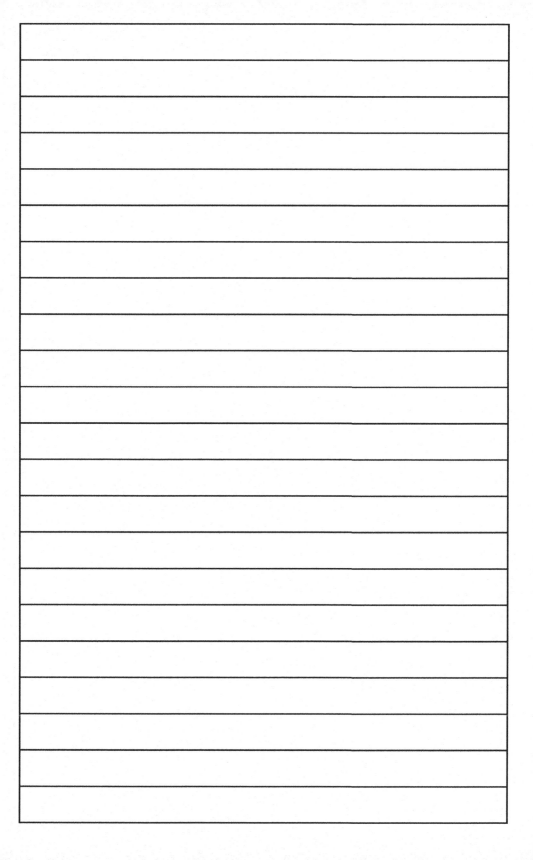

Journal Prompt:

Pretend you're a pirate. Snarl the lip, stop brushing your hair, and loudly bang around your home looking for rum. Pirates all have one thing in common... *treasure*. It's time to find hidden treasure. Make a list of 10 things in your life that you treasure.

Date:

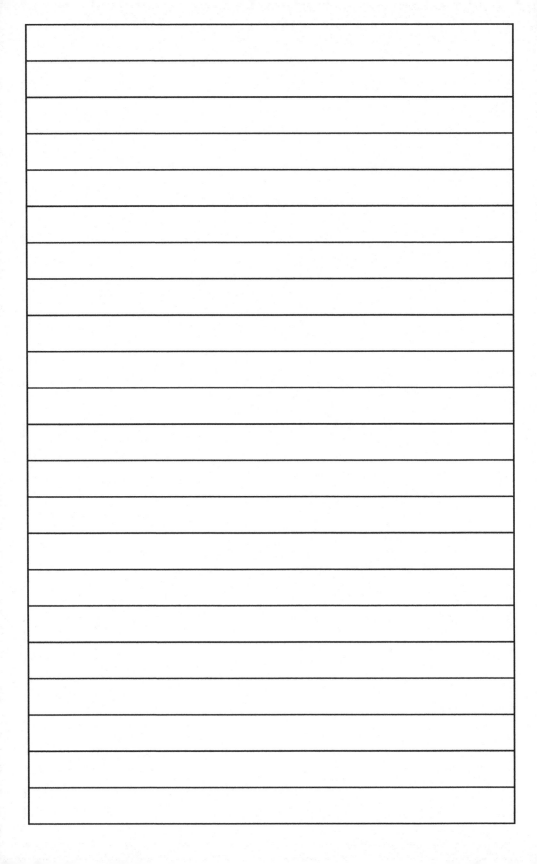

Journal Prompt:

Life sucks sometimes. Think about the last really bad day that you had. What were you the most thankful for on that day? Was it the friend that showed up to help you or the fact that you held your tongue and didn't scream at the jerk in traffic?

Date:

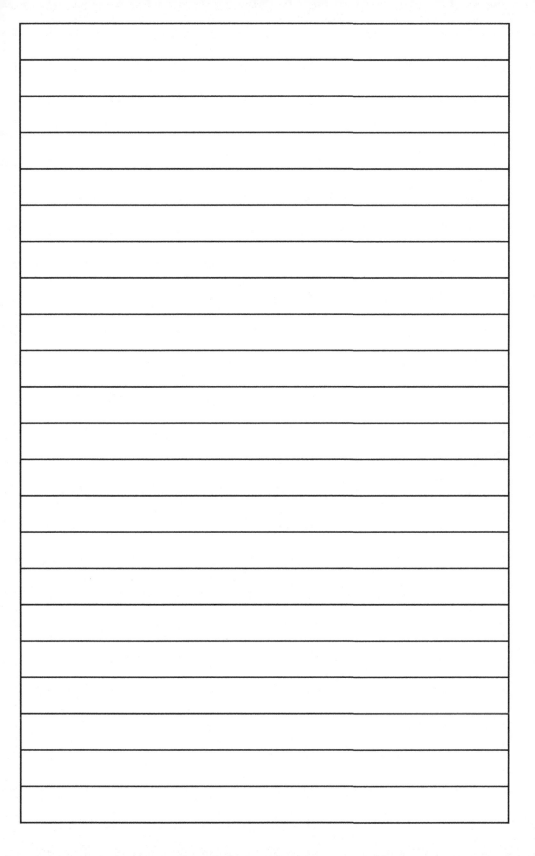

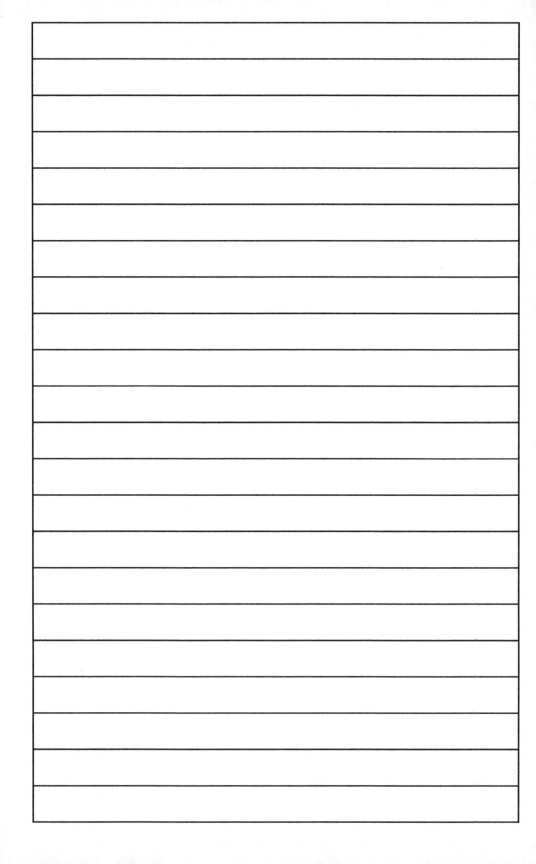

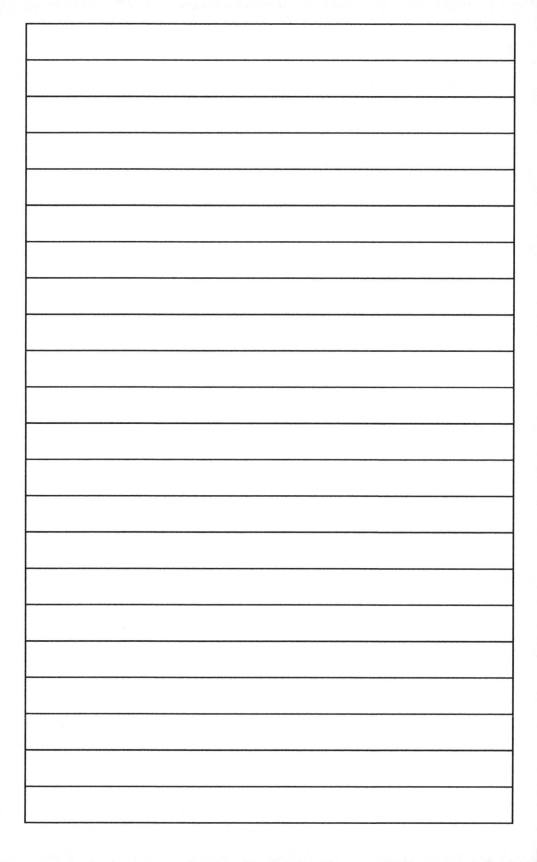

Who is your biggest cheerleader? You know... that person that waves like a lunatic in the crowd and might own a tshirt with your face on it? Don't forget - it's OK for it to be you.

Date:

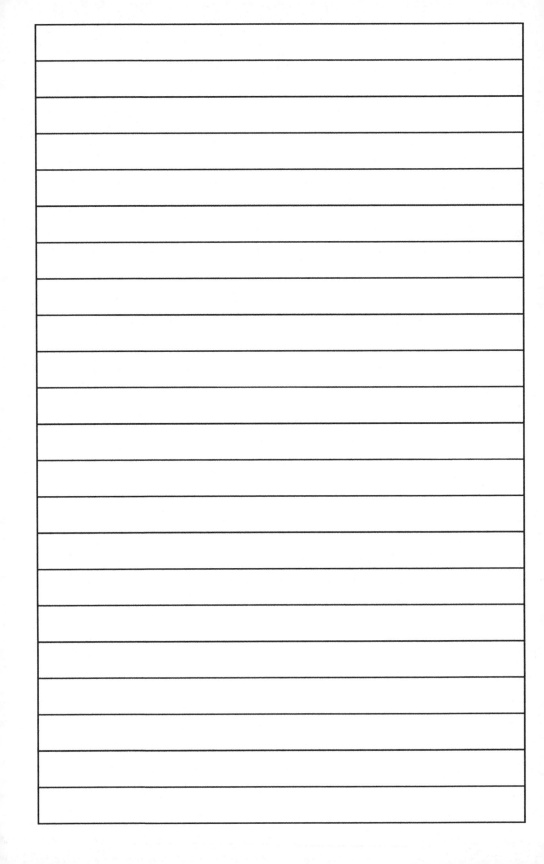

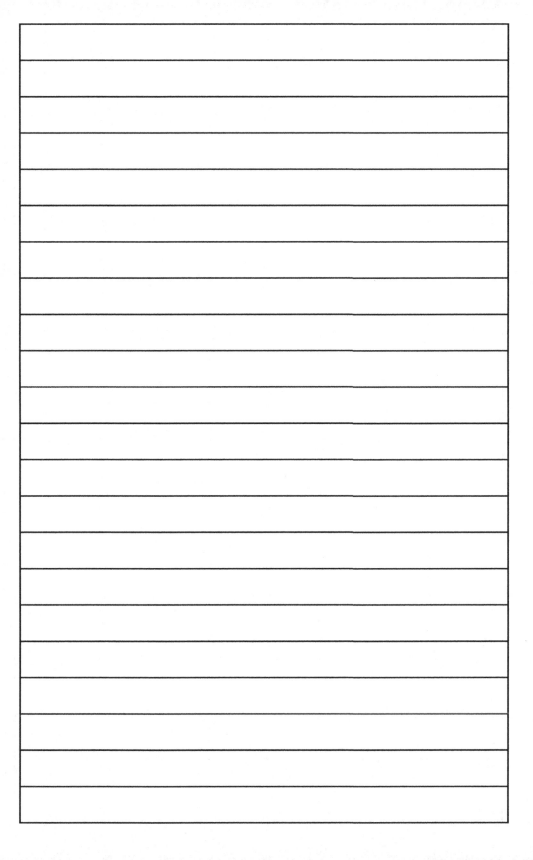

Journal Prompt:

Do a quick internet search for "gratitude quotes".
Which one catches your eye? What stands out to you
about that quote? Could you apply it to your life or
would you rather drop kick it into next week?

Date:

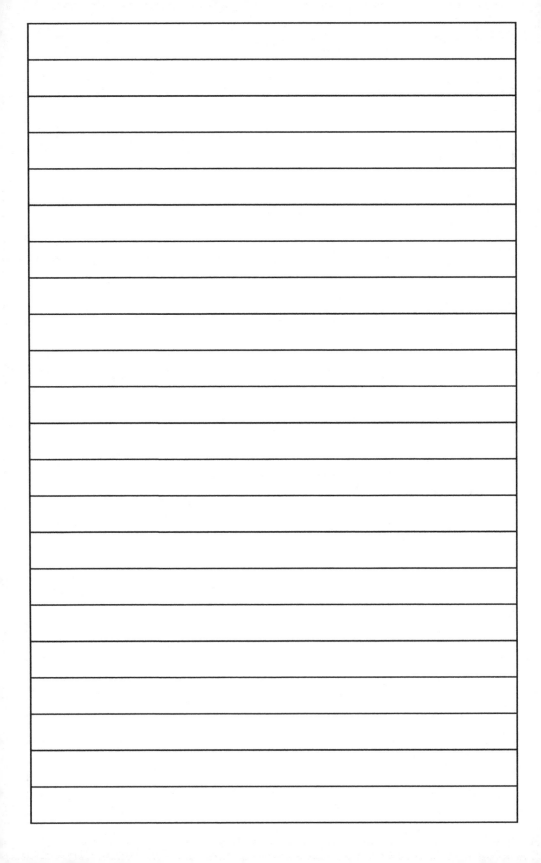

Journal Prompt:

What's the smallest goal you achieved this month?
(Getting out of bed totally counts.) Make a list of
the ten tiniest goals you've achieved lately.

Date:

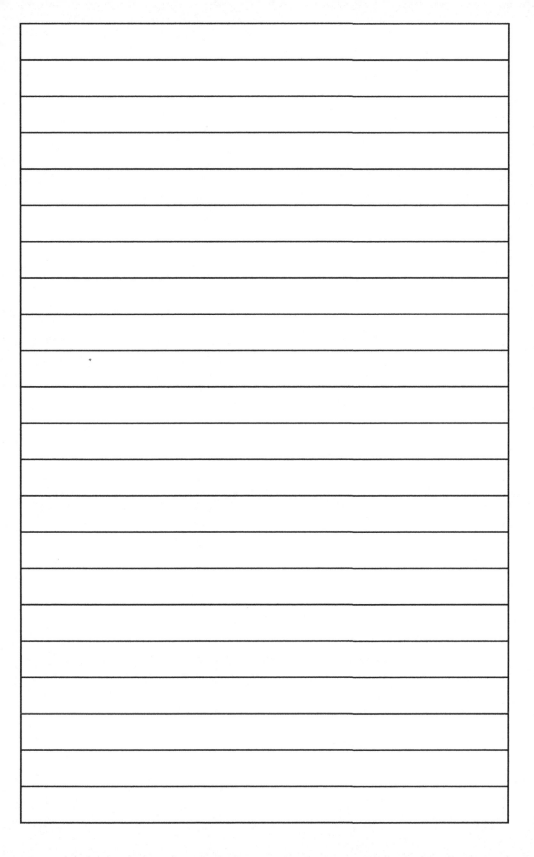

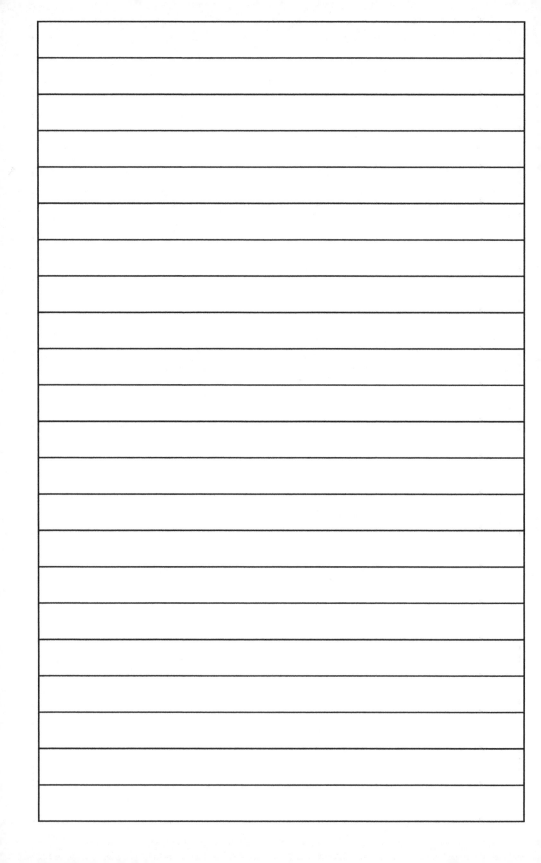

Journal Prompt:

What's your favorite season? Are you in love with spring because you can dance among the daffodils? Or do you love winter because you can pelt people with snowballs? What do you love about that season? and why are you thankful for that time of year?

Date:

Journal Prompt:

It's time to get real. Get out that mirror and get
comfy. Take a long, hard look at yourself and then
write a list of at least 3 things you like about
yourself.

Date:

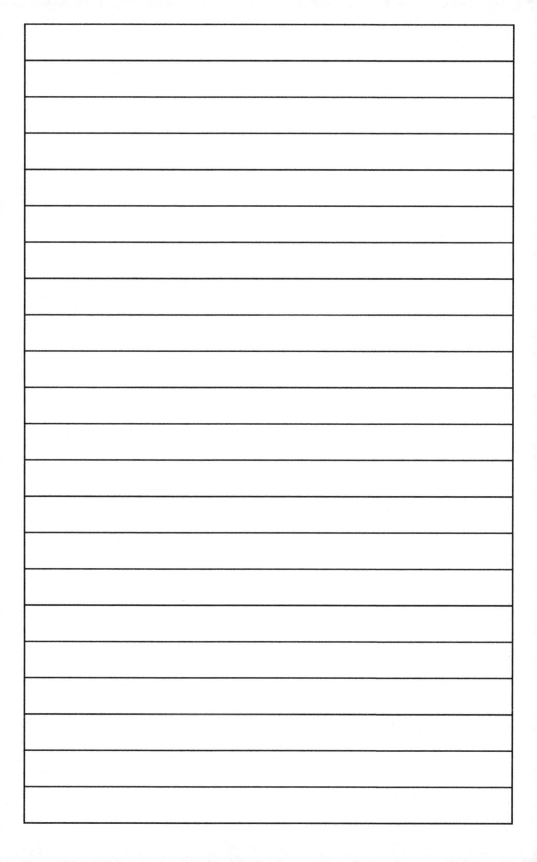

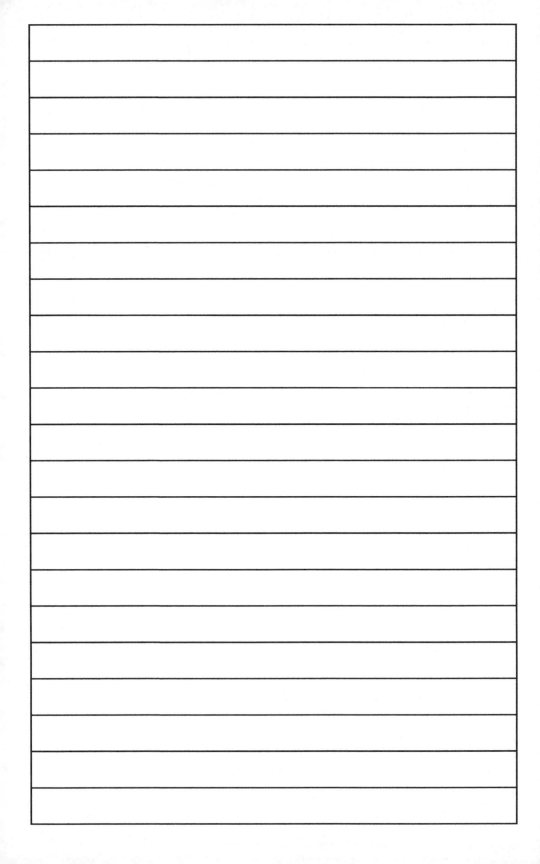

Journal Prompt:

In school they teach you that a negative plus a negative equals a positive. Maybe that's true? Or maybe it's just a load of crap. But let's give it a try. Write about something negative in your life that somehow turned into a positive.

Date:

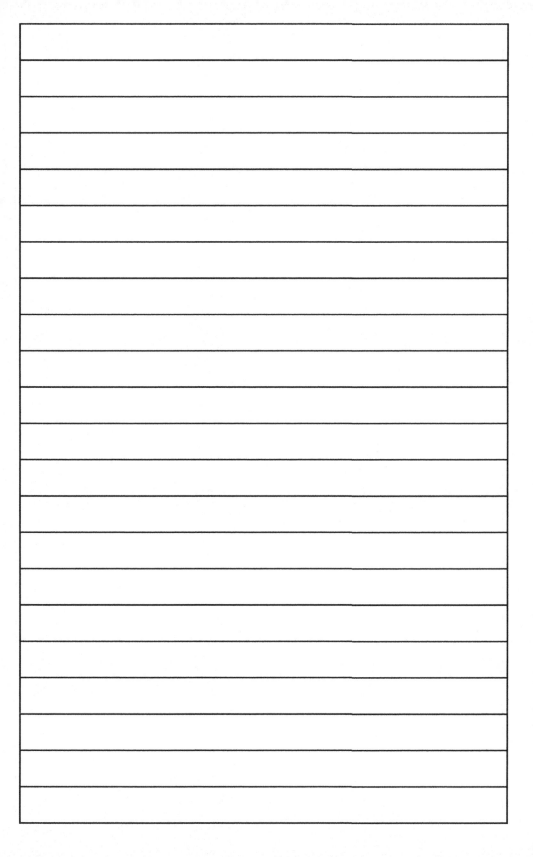

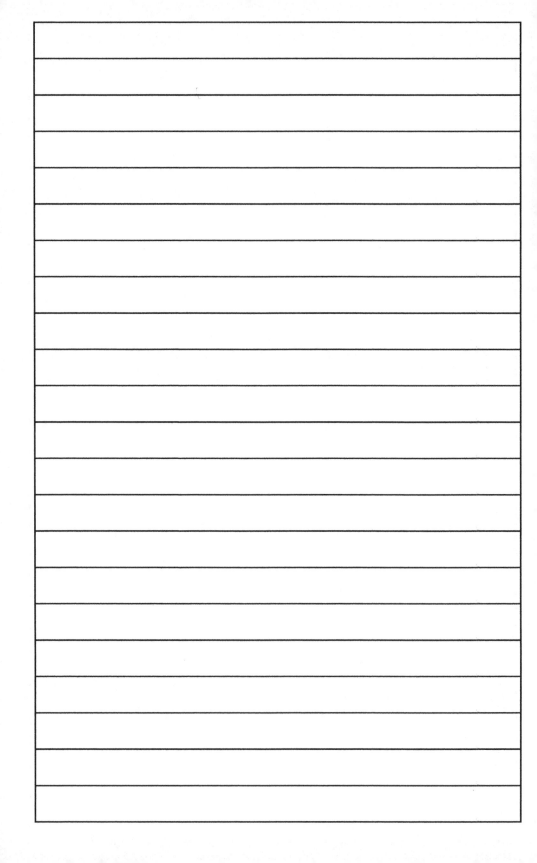

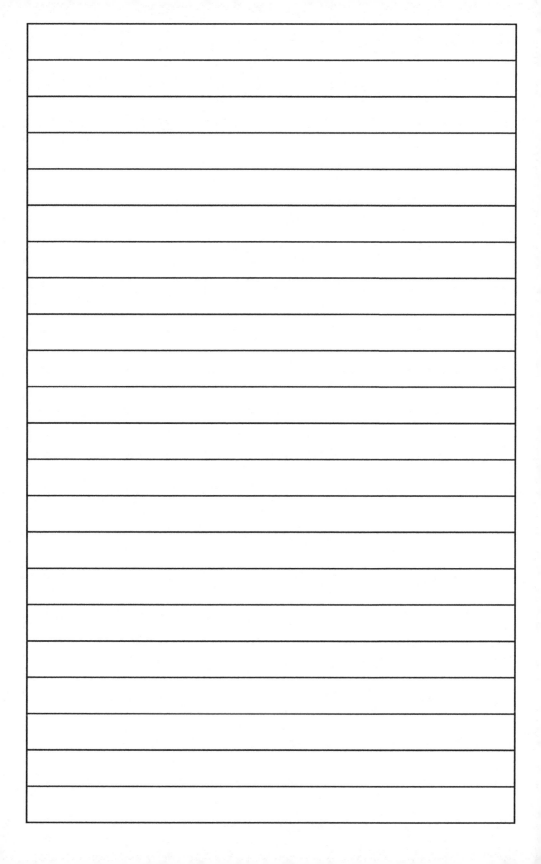

Journal Prompt:

Do you sing in the shower? *Don't lie.*
What's your favorite song to
belt out when you're happy?
What song do you listen to on repeat when you're down?
What song is your personal anthem?

Date:

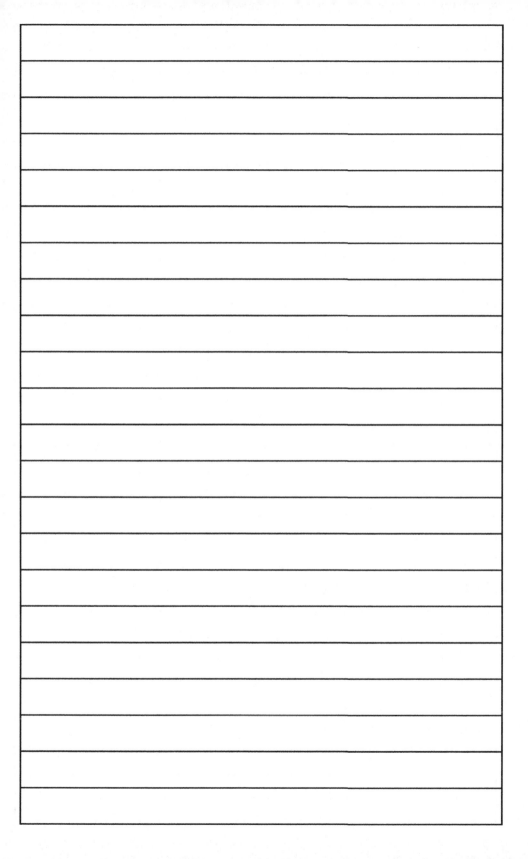

You've been challenged to a stirring game of Eye-Spy.
Look around the room. Name 5 things that bring you joy
that are in that room. No cheating.

Date:

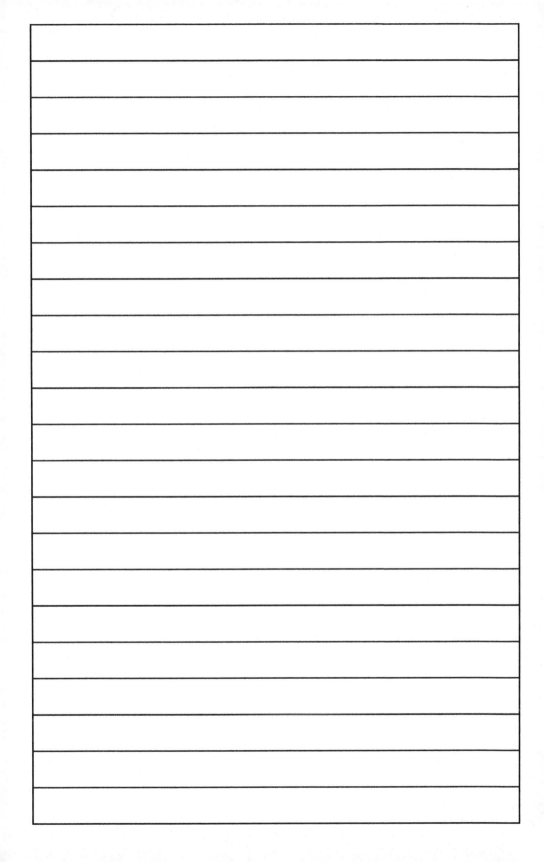

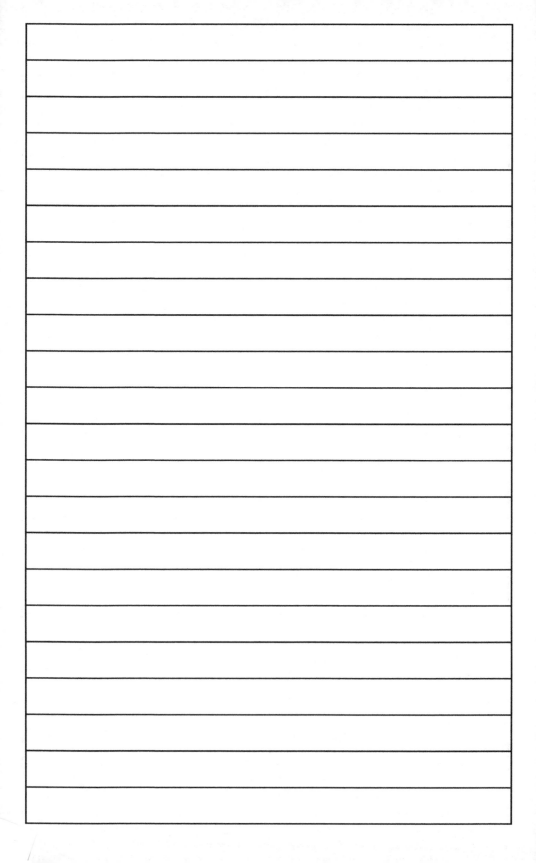

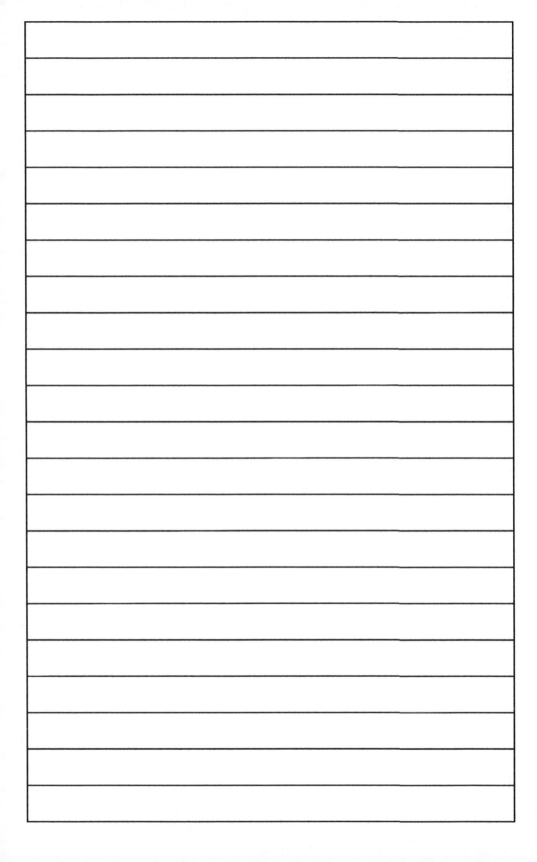

Journal Prompt:

Date:

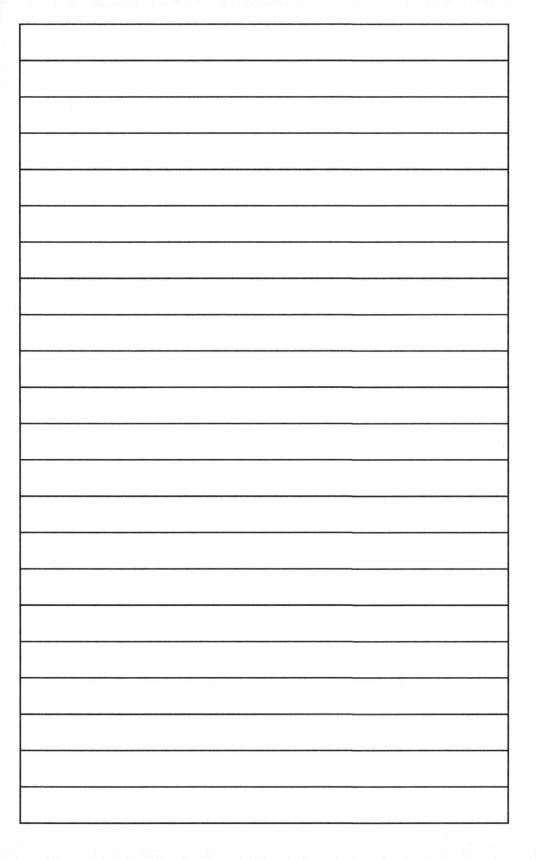

Journal Prompt:

Date:

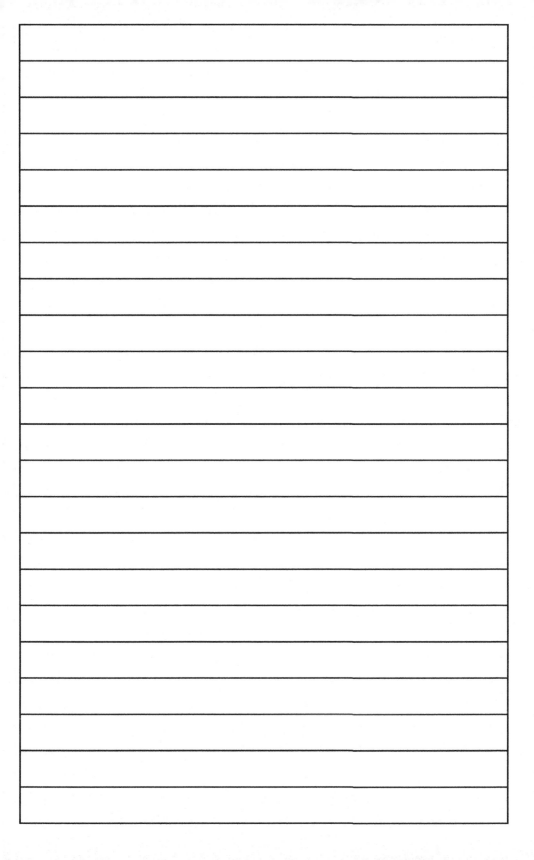

Journal Prompt:

Date:

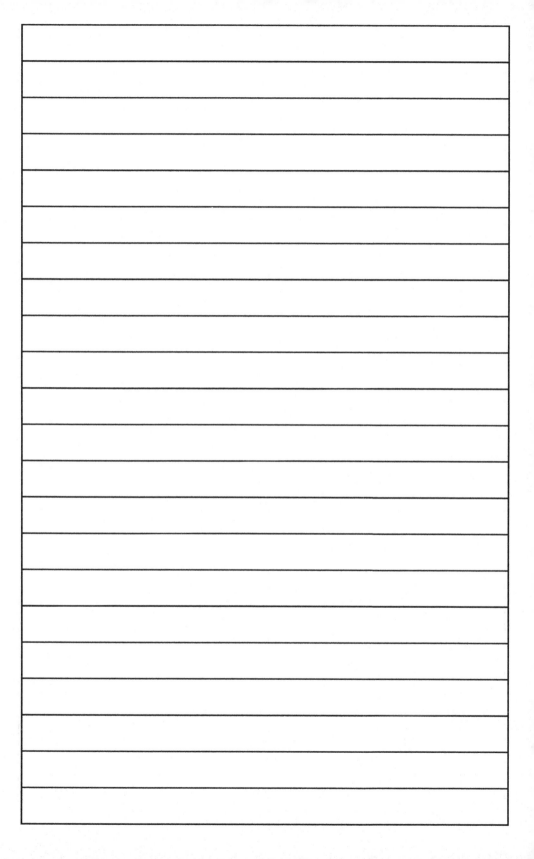

Journal Prompt:

Date:

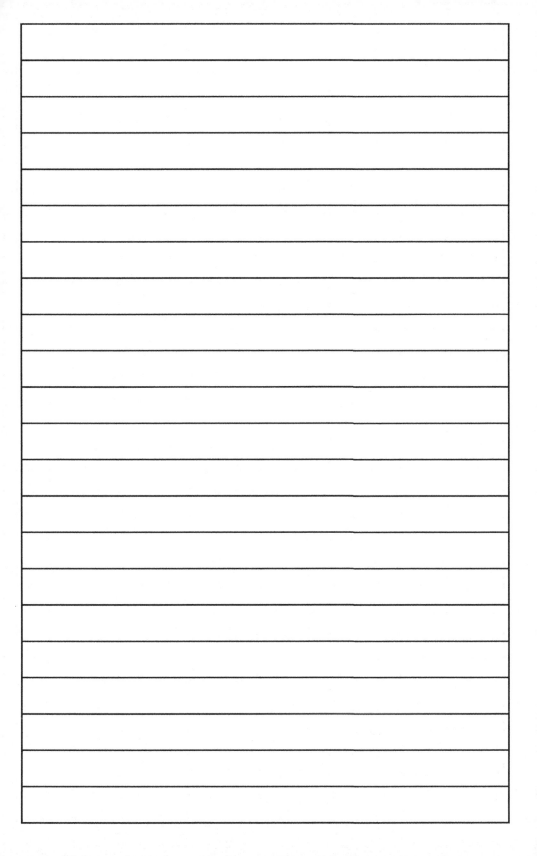

Journal Prompt:

Date:

Some people grumble that roses have thorns; I am grateful that torns have roses.

Alphonse Karr